# WALKING IN FORGIVENESS

"Bear with each other and forgive one another if any of you has a grievance against someone. Forgive as the Lord forgave you."

**Col 3:13**

By
Franklin N. Abazie

# *Walking in Forgiveness*

COPYRIGHT 2017 BY Franklin N Abazie
ISBN: 978-1-945-133-77-0

All right reserved. This book or any portion thereof may not be reproduced or used in any manner whatsoever without the express written permission of the publisher, except for the use of brief quotations in a book review. All Bible quotes are from King James Version and others as noted.

Published by: F N ABAZIE PUBLISHING HOUSE---
a.k.a,
Empowerment Bookstore:

That I may publish with the voice of thanksgiving and tell of all thy wondrous works. **Psalms26:7**

To order additional copies, wholesales or booking: Call the Church office (973-372-7518)
or Empowerment Bookstore Hotline 973-393-8518
Worship address:
343 Sanford Avenue Newark New Jersey 07106
Administrative Head Office address:
33 Schley Street Newark New Jersey 07112
Email:pastorfranknto@yahoo.com
Website www.fnabaziehealingministries.org
Publishing House: www.fnabaziepublishinghouse.org

This book is a production of F N Abazie
Publishing House.

A publication Arms of Miracle of God Ministries 2017
First Edition

# CONTENTS

THE MANDATE OF THE COMMISSION.............iv

ARMS OF THE COMMISSION............................v

INTRODUCTION...................................................vi

CHAPTER 1

1. What is Forgiveness? .........................................12

CHAPTER 2

2. How do I walk in Forgiveness?..........................31

CHAPTER 3

3. Prayer of Salvation.............................................57

CHAPTER 4

4. About the Author................................................73

# *THE MANDATE OF THE COMMISSION*

"THE MOMENT IS DUE TO IMPACT YOUR WORLD THROUGH THE REVIVAL OF THE HEALING & MIRACLE MINISTRY OF JESUS CHRIST OF NAZARETH.

I AM SENDING YOU TO RESTORE HEALTH UNTO THEE AND I WILL HEAL THEE OF THY WOUNDS, SAID THE LORD OF HOST."

## *ARMS OF THE COMMISSION*

1) F N Abazie Ministries-Miracle of God Ministries (Miracle Chapel Intl)

2) F N Abazie TV Ministries: Global Television Ministry Outreach.

3) F N Abazie Radio Ministries: Radio Broadcasting Outreach.

4) F N Abazie Publishing House: Book Publication.

5) F N Abazie Bible School: also called Word of Healing Bible School (W.O.H.B.S)

6) F N Abazie Evangelistic Ass: Miracle of God Ministries: Global Crusade

7) Empowerment Bookstore: Book distribution.

8) F N Abazie Helping Hands: Meeting the help of the needy world wide

9) F N Abazie Disaster Recovery Mission: Global Disaster Recovery.

10) F N Abazie Prison Ministry: Prison Ministry for all convicts "Second chance"

**Some of our ministry arms are waiting the appointed time to commence**

# FAVOR CONFESSION

Father thank you for making me righteous and accepted through the blood of Jesus Christ. Because of that, I am blessed and highly favored by God. I am the subject of your affection. Your favor surrounds me as a shield, and the first thing that people see around me is your favored shield.

Thank you that I have favor with you and man today. All day long people go out of their way to bless me and help me. I have favor with everyone that I deal with today. Doors that were once closed are now opened for me. I receive preferential treatment, and I have special privileges, I am Gods favored child.

No good thing will he withhold from me. Because of Gods favor my enemies cannot triumph over my life. I have supernatural increase and promotion. I declare restoration to everything that the devil has stolen from my life. I have honor in the midst of my adversaries and an increase in assets, especially in real estate and expansion of territories.

Because I am highly favored by God, I experience great victories, supernatural turnarounds, and miraculous breakthrough in the midst of great impossibilities.

I receive recognition, prominence, and honor. Petitions are granted to me even by ungodly authorities. Policies, rules, regulations, and laws are changed and reverse on my behalf.

I win battles that I don't even have to fight, because God fights them for me. This is the day, the set time and the designated moment for me to experience the free favor of God, that profusely and lavishly abound on my behalf in Jesus name.

**Amen.**

# INTRODUCTION

*"For if ye forgive men their trespasses, your heavenly Father will also forgive you: But if ye forgive not men their trespasses, neither will your Father forgive your trespasses."*
**Mathew6:14-15**

In my own opinion the first step into genuine deliverance is our ability to "forgive anyone who offended us in the past."

*"For if ye forgive men their trespasses, your heavenly Father will also forgive you: But if ye forgive not men their trespasses, neither will your Father forgive your trespasses."* **Mathew 6:14-15**

Forgiveness is the act to consciously release one's self from anger, bitterness, or resentment. It our ability to free our heart from any past hurtful experience, frustration, fear, failure, blame or resentment.

Although the practice of forgiveness is an integral teaching of Jesus doctrine, not many of the so called Christians are practicing it today.

Our Heavenly father promised us that as we forgive others of their trespasses, God will forgive our own trespasses.

*"For if ye forgive men their trespasses, your heavenly Father will also forgive you: But if ye forgive not men their trespasses, neither will your Father forgive your trespasses."*

In this small book it is my desire as directed by the Holy Spirit for anyone reading to develop a more forgiving heart, especially after reading this book. As you read this small book, allow the Holy Spirit to lead and guide your heart.

If there is anyone who offended or violated you, take a few minutes and forgive them from your heart. I pray you forgive anyone, or any experience that have held or hindered you from breakthrough in your life.

# HIS DESTINY WAS THE CROSS....

# HIS PURPOSE WAS LOVE.....

# HIS REASON WAS YOU....

"For if ye forgive men their trespasses, your heavenly father will also forgive you."

**Matthew 6:14**

# CHAPTER 1
# WHAT IS FORGIVENESS?

Simply defined; Forgiveness is our ability to forgive anyone, any institution, or group of people who trespassed or violated us, in any way in life.

*"For if ye forgive men their trespasses, your heavenly Father will also forgive you: But if ye forgive not men their trespasses, neither will your Father forgive your trespasses."* **Mathew 6:14-15.**

In my own opinion, I do not consider anyone a Christian, unless they practice forgiveness as a lifestyle. Whenever we embrace forgiveness as a lifestyle, we provoke the love of God, the mercy of God, long suffering, faith, peace, hope, gratitude, and joy. These fruits of the spirits are the gateway into prosperity of the soul, spirit, and body. If you must prosper, then you must live in peace with all men, and for us to live in peace with all men, we must live in forgiveness with all men.

Chapter 1 - What is Forgiveness?

# What then is forgiveness?

Cut to the chase, forgiveness is a decision to let go of any thought of revenge.

*"Dearly beloved, avenge not yourselves, but rather give place unto wrath: for it is written, Vengeance is mine; I will repay, saith the Lord."* **Romans12:19**

The act that offended us will always remain a part of our life, but forgiveness go a long way to set the pace for fresh start or new beginning in life. Forgiveness leads into a feeling of empathy, and compassion for the one who hurt us. *"Bear with each other and forgive one another if any of you has a grievance against someone. Forgive as the Lord forgave you."* **Col3:13**

As far as I know the act of forgiveness doesn't not justify the offence or act of hurt committed. But if anyone must experience peace, the love of God, and prosperity of the spirit, soul and body in life we must embrace forgiveness as a lifestyle.

For Gods does not want us to live in bitterness. It is written *"Looking diligently lest any man fail of the grace of God; lest any root of bitterness springing up trouble you, and thereby many be defiled;"* **Hebrew12:15.**

Usually the spirit of bitterness grows with time in our heart, if we do not confront the resentment, or anger. Any hurtful offense, or heartbroken feeling, or emotional breakdown if left untreated, from the memory lane of the heart get stored like a seed.

Often most of us replay it in our minds, creating deep ruts that makes it impossible to overcome such bitterness.

Every time we rehearse any bitter feeling in our heart, we prepare our spirit man for retaliation, and revenge.

## Chapter 1 - What is Forgiveness?

It is written *"Dearly beloved, avenge not yourselves, but rather give place unto wrath: for it is written, Vengeance is mine; I will repay, saith the Lord."* **Romans 12:19**

## Know that God requires forgiveness.

The truth is Cain really did not have to kill Abel his brother. But Cain out of bitterness and frustration, killed his own brother.

*"And Abel, he also brought of the firstlings of his flock and of the fat thereof. And the Lord had respect unto Abel and to his offering: But unto Cain and to his offering he had not respect. And Cain was very wroth, and his countenance fell. And the Lord said unto Cain, Why art thou wroth? and why is thy countenance fallen? If thou doest well, shalt thou not be accepted? and if thou doest not well, sin lieth at the door. And unto thee shall be his desire, and thou shalt rule over him.*

*And Cain talked with Abel his brother: and it came to pass, when they were in the field, that Cain rose up against Abel his brother, and slew him.*

*And the Lord said unto Cain, Where is Abel thy brother? And he said, I know not: Am I my brother's keeper? And he said, What hast thou done? the voice of thy brother's blood crieth unto me from the ground."*
**Genesis 4:4-10**

Our lack of forgiveness is why we choose to hold onto bitterness, letting it ripen into full grown resentment. While it looks like we are unable to forgive, sometimes we need to face that we are unwilling.

In the parable of the man who was forgiven a great debt (Matthew 18:24-35), we see the forgiven man immediately demands payment from someone who owes him a fraction of what he himself owed.

## Chapter 1 - What is Forgiveness?

Though he was shown mercy and grace, he was unwilling to extend it even in a small way.

Understand that we are to forgive because we are forgiven.

You can discern a person is trapped when their first response is, "You don't understand what they did to me."

We may not understand, but Jesus Christ does. He lived a perfect life, but was beaten, mocked, spit on, and hung on a wooden cross to die a cruel death.

Yet, John 3:16 says that he loved the world enough to go through this. Sometimes we mistakenly think he died only for us, but when he died, he died for the world—including whoever offended you.

We are told to forgive others just as Christ forgave us. Do they deserve it? No.

Do we deserve it? Again, no. But still, he hung on that cursed tree because of his love for each of us.

When we have an unforgiving spirit, our eyes are not on him; they are fixed on ourselves. Once when I'd been hurt, I told God, "Someone should pay for this." And in his kind, loving, tender way he said to me, "I paid."

**We must always pray for those we can't forgive.**

God already knows what's going on inside of you. He knows your thoughts and he knows how the other person hurt you. He was there.

**Why is it so easy to hold a grudge?**

Whenever we are hurt by someone we love and trust, we always become angry, resentful and frustrated. Often if we dwell on hurtful events or situations, bitter feeling

## Chapter 1 - What is Forgiveness?

engulfs our heart immediately, producing anger and resentment, as the reason for vengeance and retaliation. Every time we rehearse the negative feelings we are swallowed up by our own sense of injustice.

**What are the effects of holding offenses?**

*"Then said he unto the disciples, It is impossible but that offences will come: but woe unto him, through whom they come! It were better for him that a millstone were hanged about his neck, and he cast into the sea, than that he should offend one of these little ones.*

*Take heed to yourselves: If thy brother trespass against thee, rebuke him; and if he repent, forgive him. And if he trespass against thee seven times in a day, and seven times in a day turn again to thee, saying, I repent; thou shalt forgive him."*
**Luk17:1-4**

Un-forgiveness is the breathing ground for sickness and disease, poverty and lack in life. As long as we hold on to offenses, we hinder our God ordained genuine blessing from flowing into our lives.

In my own understanding, prolonged un-forgiveness equals prolongs poverty, lack and want in anyone life. I admonish you to embrace forgiveness as a life style and watch your life take off in your next level in life.

**Learning to forgive can only help you; it cannot hurt you.**

Forgiveness is immensely practical and helpful. There is nothing vague, or impractical about it. Forgiveness sets you free. As you learn to forgive many problems (possibly even health problems) will gradually disappear. It will be as if you can view your life from above and can see the easiest way get to where you want to be.

## Chapter 1 - What is Forgiveness?

Life will open up in front of you. New opportunities will emerge as if from nowhere. Happy coincides will occur where you meet just the right person at just the right time. Ideas or answers will come to you just as you need them.

A friend may make a comment, or you flip open a book or a magazine, or you may overhear a conversation which gives you just what you were looking for.

Why is this so? It is because by practicing forgiveness you become more open to the goodness of life, so that goodness is more able to find its way to you.

As you learn to forgive, abilities which have been dormant within you will emerge, and you will discover yourself to be a much stronger and more capable person than you previously imagined.

Parts of yourself which could not thrive in the frigid soil of unforgiveness will start to grow. You will begin to let go of struggling and striving. You will find more of an easy flow and life will be a lot more pleasant and a lot more enjoyable.

If this all sounds like exaggeration, then let that be for now. Simply practice the Four Steps to Forgiveness that you will find within these pages and you will be very glad that you did.

## The Danger of Unforgiveness

Many people ruin their health and their lives by taking the poison of bitterness, resentment and unforgiveness.

*Matthew 18:23-35* tells us that if we do not forgive people, we get turned over to the torturers. If you have a problem in this area or have ever had one, I'm sure you bear witness with what I'm saying. It's torture to have hateful thoughts toward another person rolling around inside your head.

Chapter 1 - What is Forgiveness?

# Helping Yourself and Others

Who are you helping most when you forgive the person who hurt you? Actually, you're helping yourself more than the other person. I always looked at forgiving people who hurt me as being really hard.

I thought it seemed so unfair for them to receive forgiveness when I had gotten hurt. I got pain, and they got freedom without having to pay for the pain they caused. Now I realize that I'm helping myself when I choose to forgive.

I'm also helping the other person by releasing them so God can do what only He can do. If I'm in the way—trying to get revenge or take care of the situation myself instead of trusting and obeying God—He has no obligation to deal with that person.

However, God will deal with those who hurt us if we'll put them in His hands through forgiveness. The act of forgiving is our seed of obedience to His Word.

Once we've sown our seed, He is faithful to bring a harvest of blessing to us one way or another.

Another way that forgiveness helps me is that it releases God to do His work in me. I'm happier and feel better physically when I'm not filled with the poison of unforgiveness. Serious diseases can develop as a result of the stress and pressure that bitterness, resentment and unforgiveness put on a person.

Mark 11:22-26 clearly teaches us that unforgiveness hinders our faith from working. The Father can't forgive our sins if we don't forgive other people. We reap what we sow. Sow mercy, and you'll reap mercy; sow judgment, and you'll reap judgment. So do yourself a favor—and forgive.

There are still more benefits of forgiveness. Your fellowship with God flows freely when you're willing to forgive, but it gets blocked by unforgiveness. Forgiveness also keeps Satan from getting an advantage over us (see 2 Corinthians 2:10-11).

Ephesians 4:26-27 tells us not to let the sun go down on our anger or give the devil any such foothold or opportunity. Remember that the devil must have a foothold before he can get a stronghold. Do not help Satan torture you. Be quick to forgive.

I also think it's hard to hate one person but love another. It's hard to treat anybody right when our heart isn't right. Even people you want to love may be suffering from your bitterness, resentment and unforgiveness.

## How to Forgive

Would you like to become more successful at forgiving others? There are practical steps that must be taken. One time I asked the Lord why so many people want to forgive but aren't successful doing it.

And He said, "Because they aren't obeying what I tell them to do in My Word."

As I searched the Word, I found the following instructions:

1. **Decide** – You will never forgive if you wait until you feel like it. Choose to obey God and steadfastly resist the devil in his attempts to poison you with bitter thoughts. Make a quality decision to forgive, and God will heal your wounded emotions in due time *(see Matthew 6:12-14)*.

2. **Depend** – You cannot forgive without the power of the Holy Spirit. It's too hard to do on your own. If you are truly willing, God will enable you, but you must humble yourself and cry out to Him for help. In *John 20:22-23* Jesus breathed on the disciples and said, "Receive the Holy Spirit!" His next instruction was about forgiving people.

## Chapter 1 - What is Forgiveness?

Ask God to breathe the Holy Spirit on you so you can forgive those who've hurt you.

3. **Obey** – The Word tells us several things we're to do concerning forgiving our enemies:

a. Pray for your enemies and those who abuse and misuse you. Pray for their happiness and welfare *(see Luke 6:27-28)*.

As you pray, God can give them revelation that will bring them out of deception. They may not even be aware they hurt you, or maybe they're aware but are so self-centered that they don't care. Either way, they need revelation.

b. …Bless and do not curse them *(Romans 12:14)*. In the Greek to bless means "to speak well of" and to curse means "to speak evil of." You can't walk in forgiveness and be a gossip. You must stop repeating the offense.

You can't get over it if you continue to talk about it. Proverbs 17:9 says that he who covers an offense seeks love.

## Who Should Forgive?

Forgive the person who badly hurt you long ago and also the stranger who stepped on your toe unaware. Take those two extremes and forgive them in addition to everyone in between.

Forgive quickly. The quicker you do it, the easier it is. Forgive freely. *Matthew 10:8* says, …Freely you have received, freely give. Forgive means "to excuse a fault, absolve from payment, pardon, send away, cancel, and bestow favor unconditionally."

When you forgive, you must cancel the debt. Do not spend your life paying and collecting debts. Hebrews 10:30 says that vengeance belongs to the Lord; He'll repay and settle the cases of His people.

## Chapter 1 - What is Forgiveness?

Let God pay you for past injustices. Do not try to collect from the people who hurt you, because the people who hurt you can't pay you

Also, forgive yourself for past sins and hurts you have caused others. You can't pay people back, so ask God to.

Forgive God if you are angry with Him because your life didn't turn out the way you thought it should. God is always just. There may be things you don't understand, but God loves you, and people make a serious mistake when they don't receive help from the only One who can truly help them.

You may even need to forgive a situation or an object—the post office, bank, a certain store that may have cheated you, a car that always gave you trouble, etc. Get rid of all poison that comes from bitterness, resentment and unforgiveness.

And remember Proverbs 4:23: Keep and guard your heart with all vigilance...for out of it flow the springs of life.

Unforgiveness is spiritual filthiness, so get washed in the water of God's Word to forgive and stay clean.

# CHAPTER 2

# HOW DO I WALK IN FORGIVESS?

To walk in forgiveness we must walk in love as a lifestyle.

It is written *"And we have known and believed the love that God hath to us. God is love; and he that dwelleth in love dwelleth in God, and God in him."* **1John4:16**

Reflect on the facts of the situation, how you've reacted, and how this combination has affected your life, health and well-being. We must always be proactively to forgive the person who's offended us in any way.

Move away from your role as victim and release the control and power the offending person and situation have had in your life

As you let go of grudges, you'll no longer define your life by how you've been hurt. You might even find compassion and understanding.

In the subconscious memory, an offense that was committed against us, or some pain that we caused others, can replay in our minds, causing continual resentment, anger, or remorse. Unless there is a genuine salvation experience no man or woman can easily forgive anyone of their trespasses. "

Forgiveness, by contrast, allows one to focus on more positive thoughts and relationships. "It allows you to free up the real estate in your brain" taken up by negative thinking.

You benefit immensely when you choose to forgive and so does everyone around you.

Whether you need to forgive others, or need to forgive yourself, doing so sets you free from the past and enables you to fulfil your true potential.

## Chapter 2 - How do I walk in Forgiveness?

Forgiveness allows you to break free from limiting beliefs and attitudes. It frees up your mental and emotional energies so that you can apply them to creating a better life.

Forgiveness helps you achieve even your most practical and immediate goals. Perhaps you want a better job, to earn more money, have better relationships, or live in a nicer place.

Forgiveness helps you achieve all of these. If you have not forgiven then a part of your inner life energy is trapped in resentment, anger, pain, or suffering of some kind. This trapped life energy will limit you. It it like trying to ride a bicycle with the brakes partly on all the time. It slows you down, frustrates you and makes it difficult to move forward.

The choices you make and the things that you believe are possible will all be influenced by the ways you have not forgiven. As you learn to forgive the energy which was going into unhappy thoughts and feelings gets liberated and can flow into creating the life you want rather than limiting you, or creating more suffering.

If you do not want to learn to forgive to benefit yourself; then learn to forgive so you can benefit others. As you learn to forgive you benefit everyone you are in contact with.

Your thinking will be clearer and more positive than before. You will have a lot more to give and you will more readily enjoy sharing what you have. You will naturally and easily become kinder, more generous and more caring of others – without having to struggle to achieve this.

You will have a happier and more positive attitude to the people in your life and they will respond more positively to you in return.

Is a forgiving person easier to be around than an unforgiving one? Yes, of course they are.

## Chapter 2 - How do I walk in Forgiveness?

A forgiving person is always much easier to be around than an unforgiving one. The quality of your life depends on the quality of your relationships. Every aspect of your life will change for the better as you learn to forgive; whether in your family, your work life or your social life.

Learning to forgive will improve all your relationships, because your attitude will improve. As your relationships improve, then all aspects of your life will also improve.

If you want to move up to the next level of financial abundance and success, Forgiveness will help you achieve it.

For example, if you want more money in your life you need to make sure that you do not resent people who have more money than you. People with more money than you are the ones best placed to help you have more money too. If, as some people do, you resent "people with money" then they will not be able to help you, because you are not open to them while you are busy resenting them.

Likewise, if you have a positive attitude to people who are more successful than you (you smile at them rather than glower at them) they will see you as approachable and will more likely want to work with you, or socialise with you.

If you want a better job, and to earn more money, then having a positive attitude towards the place you work, towards your boss, towards colleagues and towards clients or customers, helps immensely. People who have a positive, helpful attitude stand out in any situation.

You can never succeed in an organization which you do not want to succeed, because you will not give of your best. If you do not give of your best, by doing the best job you can, then you will not receive the best that can come to you. Forgiveness will help you have the kind of attitude which will make you very successful at your job.

Learning to forgive yourself is vitally important too.

## Chapter 2 - How do I walk in Forgiveness?

Hurting yourself, by refusing to forgive yourself, hurts others also. If you do not forgive yourself then you will punish yourself by denying yourself the good things in life. The more you deny yourself the less you have to give.

The less you have to give the less you can benefit those around you. When you stop limiting what you receive then you stop limiting what you can give. Everyone benefits when you forgive yourself as you then allow more good into your life, and have a lot more to share.

When you forgive; you become a better husband or wife, you become a better student or teacher, you become a better employer or employee and you become a better parent or child. When you forgive you are more open to success in whatever ways are meaningful to you. As you learn to forgive, what seemed impossible not only becomes possible, but can even become easily achievable.

If you are a religious, or spiritually minded, person then learning practical ways to forgive will enhance and deepen your experience of your religion or spiritual practice. It will help free you from guilt about not being as "good" as you feel you should be, because it will help you become the type of person you would like to be.

Practising forgiveness strengthens the goodness within you so that it becomes more active in your life. You will naturally feel less inclined to do the things you know you should not do, but have not been able to stop yourself doing. You will start to do more of the things you know you ought to do, but have not been able to get yourself to do.

## Why can't I overcome my bitterness and anger?

Most of our bitterness and anger towards others is rooted in an inability to be profoundly amazed at Christ's love for us in our sin.

## Chapter 2 - How do I walk in Forgiveness?

If you are struggling with bitterness then it may be that the Lord is letting the very sin that is flowing from your inability to see Christ be the means by which you come to see him.

In other words, perhaps this season of rage, anger, and a fed-up "I'm out of here and don't want anything to do with you" spirit is where you have had to come in order to see the greatness of your sin as a forgiven and justified saint.

And the Lord has done it so that you would be stunned at his grace in a deeper way than you've ever been stunned by the grace of God before. And now, out of that experience can flow grace towards others.

That's the only solution here. I don't doubt that another person is part of the problem. This is probably not just a one-way thing and your fault only. But the solution is not to fix the other person.

The solution is to gain a heart that is overflowingly thankful for grace from Christ and that spills over with grace towards others.

What I'm trying to draw attention to is that maybe God has brought you to this point of feeling your guilt so that grace would taste sweeter than it ever has. We have to see our sin, but some of us have grown up in such goody-goody homes that we don't think we've ever done anything serious.

But unforgiveness is a hell-bent sin. The Bible says that if you do not forgive those who sin against you, God will not forgive you *(Matthew 6:15)*.

In other words, this is a mortal issue. An ongoing, unforgiving, bitter, and angry spirit will kill a person's heart, making them shipwreck their faith and prove that they never belonged to God. God is showing you how serious this sin is.

## Chapter 2 - How do I walk in Forgiveness?

This means that now you have the potential of saying, "If he loves me still, and he forgives this, it's like forgiving the apostle Paul!" (It's like forgiving murderers, because the Bible says that if you hate your brother you've killed him *[Matthew 5:21-22]*.

And then maybe the emotional transaction of forgiveness and justification would so overwhelm you that the resources that you do not now have for loving this other person would be given you out of that fresh, new experience of grace.

That's what I would pray. "Forgive one another, as God in Christ forgave you" is an unbelievably important word in Ephesians 4:32. You now have the potential of feeling forgiven by God for things that are mortally dangerous, which might open the door for greater grace towards this other person.

## CONCLUSION

*"Though he slay me, yet will I trust in him: but I will maintain mine own ways before him."* **Job13:15**

Unless otherwise stated, we must all come unto repentance if we must encounter our savior Jesus Christ. Repentance is the key to deliverance, protection, and promotion. Everyone that desired to encounter testimonies in their prayer must confess and forsake their sinful ways and go after God.

*"Let us hear the conclusion of the whole matter: Fear God, and keep his commandments: for this is the whole duty of man.*

*For God shall bring every work into judgment, with every secret thing, whether it be good, or whether it be evil."*
**Eccl12:13-14**

The entire book will remain a story to everyone who is not ready to make a

## Chapter 2 - How do I walk in Forgiveness?

decision for Jesus Christ. One man said if you failed to plan we have planned to fail in life. We want you to make plans to make heaven.

The bible says in eccl: 12:14 For God shall bring every work into judgment, with every secret thing, whether it be good, or whether it be evil. If you are a born again Christian; we like to encourage you in your Christian life. If you are not a born again Christian we can help you here receive genuine salvation.

*"Therefore if any man be in Christ, he is a new creature: old things are passed away; behold, all things are become new."*
**2cor5:17**

## Now repeat this Prayer after me

Say Lord Jesus, I accept you today, as my Lord and my savior, forgive me of my sins wash me with your blood. Right now, I believe, I am sanctified, I am save, I am free, I am free from the Power of sin to serve the Lord Jesus. Thank you Lord for saving me. Amen.

## Congratulations:

**YOU ARE NOW A BORN AGAIN CHRISTIAN**

**AGAIN I SAY TO YOU CONGRATULATION**

## Chapter 2 - How do I walk in Forgiveness?

# What must I do to determine my divine visitation?

## To determine divine visitation you must be born again

The word says as many as received him, to them gave He power to become the sons of God. Even to them that believe on his name.

To qualify for divine visitation do the following sincerely

1) Acknowledge that you are a sinner and that He died for you. **Rom3:23.**

2) Repent of your sins. **Acts 3:19, Luke13:5, 2Peter3:9**

3) Believe in your heart that Jesus died for your sin. **Romans10:10**

4) Confess Jesus as the Lord over your life. **Romans10:10, Acts2:21**

**Now repeat this Prayer after me**

Say Lord Jesus, I accept you today, as my Lord and my savior, forgive me of my sins wash me with your blood. Right now, I believe, I am sanctified, I am save, I am free, I am free from the Power of sin to serve the Lord Jesus. Thank you Lord for saving me. Amen.

### Congratulation:

## YOU ARE NOW A BORN AGAIN CHRISTAIN

## AGAIN I SAY TO YOU CONGRATULATION

I adjure you to watch the Spirit of God bear witness with your Spirit confirming His word with signs following. The word says The Spirit itself beareth witness with our spirit, that we are the children of God.

Join a bible believing church or join us on our weekly and Sunday worship services at 343 Sanford Avenue Newark New Jersey 07106

Chapter 2 - How do I walk in Forgiveness?

# WISDOM KEYS

Every Productive Society is a society heading to the top

Millions of Nigerians run away from Nigeria, very few Nigerians stay in Nigeria.

My decision to return Nigeria is the will of God for my life

My short coming in America after 18 years, trained me to be wise, to think, reflect and reason appropriately.

If you train your mind to reason it will train your hands to earn money.

It is absurd to use the money of the heathen to build the kingdom of the living God.

Every Ministry reveals its agenda and goal either at the beginning or at the end. Be careful of your life it is your first Ministry.

The average American mind is conditioned for a continual quest to get new things and (discard the former) and throw away old things.

When I considered well, my BMW jeep became my initial deposit for the work of the ministry in Nigeria

Everyone is waiting for you to change your mind until you change your thinking nothing changes around you.

Multiple academic degrees in other discipline gave me the chance to think, reflect and reason

What so everyone are thinking and reflecting at the moment reveals you to the time and the now factor

All events and intents are the product of precise thought processes, accurate reason every event is designed for a designated timeline

Wisdom is your ability to think, to create and invent. If you can think wise enough you will come out of penury

The distance between you and success is your creative ability to think reason and reflect accurate.

## Chapter 2 - How do I walk in Forgiveness?

Success is the result of hard work, commitment resolve and determination learning from past mistakes and failing.

If you organize your mind you have organized your life and destiny.

There is a thin line between success and failure. If you look above and beyond you are on your way to success.

Wealth is your ability to think, power is your ability to reason and success is your ability to be informed.

If you can make use of your mind by thinking and reasoning God will make use of your life and destiny.

Think and Be Great

Reflect, Reason, think and be great

Famous people are born of woman

That you will make it is your intention; that you will survive is your resolve, that you will succeed with changes is your determination, personal efforts and hard work.

No man was born a failure. Lack of vision is the end product of failure.

Working with mental patients encourages and aspire me to be a productive observant and dedicated to my assignment.

Successful people are not magicians, it is the will power combined with hard work, and determination and a resolve to succeed that make them succeed.

In the unequivocal state of the mind, intention is not a location or a position it is the state of the mind.

So many people think that they think. The mind is used to think reflect and reason. You will remain blind with your eye open until you can see with your mind by thinking.

There is no favoritism in accurate and precise calculation

## Chapter 2 - How do I walk in Forgiveness?

Although knowledge is power, information is the key and gateway to a great future.

It will take the hand of God to move the hand of man.

With the backing of the great wise God, nothing will disconnect you from your inheritance.

As long as you have wisdom and understanding of God, Satan and evil cannot manipulate your life and destiny.

You have come this far by yourself judgment and decision you have made in the past, now lean and listen to God for another dimension of greatness.

Great people are common people it is extra ordinary effort and the price of sacrifice that produces greatness.

As a mental direct care worker I saw a great pastor and a motivational speaker within myself.

Menial job does not reduce your self-worth, until you resolve to achieve greatness see greatness in all you do; you will never count in your community

The principle of Jesus will solve your gambling and addiction problems

The man of Jesus will lead you into heaven,

Everyone have their self-appraisal and what they think about you. Until you discover yourself other opinion about you will alter the real you.

Supervisors and directors are just a position in the chain of command in a work place. Never allow your supervisor hierarchy to alter your opinion about yourself.

Everyone can come out of debt if they make up their mind.

That I am not a decision maker at work does not diminish my contribution to my world.

Although it appears like it was a poor decision to accept a direct care employment at a psychiatric hospital as I reflect of my nine years of experience, it became apparent that I have learnt and experienced enough for my next assignment.

Self-encouragement and determination is a resolve of the heart.

## Chapter 2 - How do I walk in Forgiveness?

If you are determined to make a difference, and do the things that make a difference you will eventually make a difference.

Good things do not come easy

Short cuts will cut your life short.

Those who look ahead move ahead.

Life is all about making an impact. In your life time strive to make an impact in your community.

Make friends and connect with people who are moving ahead of you in life.

If you can look around well you have come a long way in your life, made a lot of difference and realized a lot of success in life.

If you are my old friend, hurry up to reach out to me before I become a stranger to you.

Everything I am blessed with inspirations from God, that change my definition and interpretation of the world around me.

I thought I was stagnant and lonely until I looked around and noticed my children running around and my wife cooking.

At 40 I resigned my Job to seek the Lord forever.

My ministry took a drastic rise to the top when the wisdom of God visited me with knowledge and understanding.

You will be a better person if you understand the characteristics of your personality – your mood swings attitudes and habits.

It is the seed of love you sow into the heart of a child and a woman that you reap in due time.

Love is not selfish, love share everything including the concealed secrets of the mind.

As long as you have a prayer life and a bible; you will never feel lonely, rejected and idle in the race of life.

When good friends disconnect from you, let them go, they might have seen something new in a different direction.

Confidence in yourself and in God is the only way to bring you out of captivity

Never train a child to waste his/her time.

The mind is the greatest assets of a great future.

## Chapter 2 - How do I walk in Forgiveness?

You walk by common sense run by principles and fly by instruction.

Those who fly in flight of life fly alone.

Up in the air you are alone. No one can toll you accept the compass of knowledge and information

I have seen a tolling vehicle I have seen a tolling ship I have never seen a tolling airplane.

I exercise my judgment and make a decision every minute of the day.

Decisions are crucial, critical and vital with reference to your future.

So many people wish for a great future. You can only work towards a great future.

Your celebrity status began when you discovered your talent. What are you good at? Work at it with all commitment.

Prayers will sustain you but the wisdom of God will prosper you.

When I met Oyedepo, his teachings changed my perspective, but when I met Ibiyeomie; His teaching changed my perception.

I will be successful in ministry if only I concentrate and focus my energy in the work of the ministry.

It took the late Dr. Vincent Pearle Norman's book to open my mind towards kingdom success.

# CHAPTER 3
# PRAYER OF SALVATION

*"Neither is there salvation in any other: for there is none other name under heaven given among men, whereby we must be saved."* **Acts 4:12**

### -Stages of Salvation-

Justification is when the soul is set free from the penalty of sin.

*"If we confess our sins, he is faithful and just and will forgive us our sins and purify us from all unrighteousness."* **1 John 1:9**

Sanctification is when the soul is set free from the power of sin.

*"For this is the will of God, even your* sanctification."
**John 17:17**

Glorification is when the soul is set free from the possibility of sin.

*"Dear friends, now we are children of God, and what we will be has not yet been made known. But we know that when he appears, we shall be like him."*

**1 John 1:3**

We enter the door of sanctification the moment we consecrate our lives to Christ and submit ourselves to the process of becoming more like him. Justification and sanctification are pre-requisites for glorification when salvation is finally complete. Glorification occurs after the death of the body when the soul is transported beyond the reach of temptation and sin.

Salvation is not complete until we have been glorified. Philippians 1:6 says, *"He who has started a good work in you will carry it on to completion."*

But, God seems to have tempered his own sovereignty by gifting man with free will.

## Chapter 3 - Prayer of Salvation

Christians are certainly eternally secure, but this security is conditional. It could be disrupted by the sovereignty of God or the free will God has given man. Can a man lose his salvation? I don't think so.

Romans 8:38 says, *"For I am convinced that nothing can ever separate us from God's love."*

Paul goes on to list all of the things that are incapable of separating us from God's love. But, Paul does not include ourselves in that list. Can a man choose to become an apostate? The Bible seems to indicate that a man can choose to walk away from God.

There are at least 80 passages of in the New Testament that teach that the process of salvation can be interrupted, delayed or stopped altogether. Jude 21 says, *"keep yourselves in God's love"* and Jude 24 says, *"He is able to keep you."*

This seems to indicate a conditional relationship. He will keep us if we will determine to be kept.

Jesus declared himself to be the true vine. Dead branches are cut away and destroyed while fruitful branches are pruned so they will produce even more fruit (John 15:4).

Christ warns against the prevalent teaching of cheap grace.

Hebrews 10:26-27 says, *"If we deliberately keep on sinning after we have received the knowledge of the truth, no sacrifice for sins is left, but only a fearful expectation of judgment and of raging fire that will consume the enemies of God."*

1 Peter 2:20 says, *"It would have been better for them not to have known the way of righteousness, than to have known it and then to turn their backs on the sacred command that was passed on to them."*

Peter is saying that people who enter the way and then departed from it are worse off.

## Chapter 3 - Prayer of Salvation

This is contradictory for those who argue that we might continue to live a sinful lifestyle and still be rewarded with eternal life. If they received eternal life how are they worse off?

One is tempted to question the idea that we cannot walk away from God because it seems to make God inconsistent. Either he has gifted us with free will or he has not. But I argue that it is very unlikely that a man would choose to walk away from God if he were truly, genuinely saved.

Maybe a more accurate statement would be not so much, "once saved always saved" but "if saved always saved."

## What must I do to determine my salvation?

To be saved we must be born again! The word says as many as received him, to them gave He power to become the sons of God. Even to them that believe on his name.

To qualify for divine visitation do the following sincerely

1) Acknowledge that you are a sinner and that He died for you. **Rom3:23.**

2) Repent of your sins. **Acts 3:19, Luke13:5, 2Peter3:9**

3) Believe in your heart that Jesus died for your sin. **Romans10:10**

4) Confess Jesus as the Lord over your life. **Romans10:10, Acts2:21**

**Now repeat this Prayer after me**

Say Lord Jesus, I accept you today, as my Lord and my savior, forgive me of my sins wash me with your blood. Right now, I believe, I am sanctified, I am save, I am free, I am free from the Power of sin to serve the Lord Jesus. Thank you Lord for saving me. Amen.

## Chapter 3 - Prayer of Salvation

**Congratulations:**

**YOU ARE NOW A BORN AGAIN CHRISTIAN**

**AGAIN I SAY TO YOU CONGRATULATIONS**

I adjure you to watch the Spirit of God bear witness with your Spirit confirming His word with signs following. The word says The Spirit itself beareth witness with our spirit, that we are the children of God.

# MIRACLE CARE OUTREACH

*"...But that the members should have the same care one for another"* **1cor12:25**

We are all members of the body of Christ. Jesus commanded us to love our neighbor as ourselves. This includes caring for one another as a member of one body. True love is expressed in caring and giving. The word says for God so Love He gave….

Reach out to someone in need of Jesus, help someone in crisis find Christ. Look out and prove your love to Jesus by caring and inviting your friends and associates to find Jesus the Healer.

Invite your friends to our Home Care Cell Fellowship (Miracle chapel Intl Satellite fellowship) In the USA at 33 Schley Street Newark New Jersey 07112.

**If you are in Nigeria—MIRACLE OF GOD MINISTRIES**

**A.K.A "MIRACLE CHAPEL INTL" Mpama –Egbu-Owerri Imo state Nigeria.**

(Home Care Cell fellowship Group). We meet every Tuesday at 6:00pm-7:00pm.

## Chapter 3 - Prayer of Salvation

# LIFE IS NOT ALL ABOUT DURATION BUT ITS ALL ABOUT DONATION

### What does the above statement mean?....

*"Life consists not in accumulation of material wealth."* **Luke12:15.**

But it's all about liberality….meaning-
*"what you can give and share with others."* **Proverb11:25.**

When you live for others--You live forever- because you out live your generation by the legacy you live behind after you depart into glory to be with the Lord.

But when you live to yourself - you are reduced to self—you are easily forgotten when you die and depart in glory.

Permit me to admonish you today to live your life to be a blessing to a soul connected to you today. I want you to know that so many souls are connected and looking up to you, and through you so many souls will be saved and rescued from destruction. Will you disciple someone today to find Jesus Christ?

*"As a genuine Christian; it is your duty to evangelize Jesus Christ to all you meet on your way. Jesus is still in the healing business-Jesus is still doing miracles from time of old to now. Therefore tell someone about Jesus Christ today, disciple and bring them to Church."*

**John 1:45 Philip findeth Nathanael….**

Please to prove the sincerity of your love for God today; please become a soul winner. The dignity of your Christianity is hidden in your boldness to proclaim and evangelize Jesus Christ to all you meet on your way.

There is a question mark on the integrity of your Christianity until you become a life soul winner. Invite someone to join us worship the Lord Jesus this coming Sunday.

**Amen**

Chapter 3 - Prayer of Salvation

# MIRACLE OF GOD MINISTRIES
## PILLARS OF THE COMMISSION

We Believe Preach and Practice the following,

1) We believe and preach Salvation to every living human being

2) We believe and preach Repentance and forgiveness of sins

3) We believe and preach the baptism of the Holy Spirit and Spiritual gifts

4) We believe and teach the Prosperity

5) We believe and preach Divine Healing and Miracles (Signs &Wonder)

6) We believe and preach Faith

7) We believe and Proclaim the Power of God (Supernatural)

8) We believe and Proclaim Praise& Worship to God

9) We believe and preach Wisdom

10) We believe and preach Holiness (Consecration)

11) We believe and preach Vision

12) We believe and teach the Word of God

13) We believe and teach Success

14) We believe and practice Prayer

15) We believe and teach Deliverance

**This 15 stones form the Pillars of Our Commission.**

Become part of this church family and follow this great move of God

# MY HEART FELT PRAYER FOR YOU

It is my prayer that you testify today about the goodness of the Lord. I desire for you to have an encounter with our Lord Jesus Christ.

**Now let me Pray for you:**

## Chapter 3 - Prayer of Salvation

Heavenly father may today be a day of new beginning for this precious love one. Lord God of heaven open a new chapter in the life of this precious love one reading this book today. May all their prayers be answered in the mighty name of Jesus. We thank you Jesus for hearing us. In Jesus mighty name. **Amen.**

## THE SUPERNATURAL BENEFITS OF LIVING IN FORGIVENESS.

### ~Long life

As long as you are not bitter against anyone, you will live long. It is written *"With long life will I satisfy him, and shew him my salvation."* **Psalm91:16.**

### ~Enjoy the Joy of the Lord as your strength.

As far as I know, no bitter man or woman, enjoys the Joy of the Lord. As long as you are bitter and angry, you are left to the tormentor. The bible says that the *"Joy of the Lord is our strength."* **Nehimiah8:10.**

Anyone without the Joy of the Lord as their strength is heading into defeat and destruction against our adversary-the devil. The Joy of the Lord becomes our strength only when we operate in forgive.

**~Healthy life**

As long as you are not bitter, you carry a merry heart. And we all know that a merry *heart doeth good like medicine.*

*It is written "A merry heart doeth good like a medicine: but a broken spirit drieth the bones."* **Prover17:22.**

We were told that "The spirit of a man will sustain his infirmity; but a wounded spirit who can bear? As long as you are bitter, you are wounded. And if you are wounded, bros, you are sick to a degree.

**~ Access into Divine Ideas**

As far as I know, no angry or bitter man have access into divine ideas. Most bitter people, converts the anointing for divine ideas into annoyance. Esau lost his lot forever because he was bitter and Jacob, and for the most part only wanted to revenge and kill Jacob.

*"And Esau hated Jacob because of the blessing wherewith his father blessed him: and Esau said in his heart, The days of mourning for my father are at hand; then will I slay my brother Jacob."* **Genesis27:41**

### ~Walking in forgiveness is a gift from God.

So many of us claim to be strong rooted Christians, yet we end up in road rage. I have had numerous encounters where descent men decided to fight not to give the lane at the entrance of the Lincoln tunnel. Into Manhattan.

To forgive or give up a fight does not mean, you are a weak person. God wants us all to live in peace and love. No man can live in peace and love without embracing forgiveness as a lifestyle.

This small book will not make sense to me, unless after reading you decide to chance some strong bitter habits about you. During a recent visit into Lagos-Nigeria, I discovered that almost everybody is very angry and bitter.

Even those of whom I hold in high esteem disappointed me by the way they react to others around them.

Our Christianity have no genuine bearing with the Holy Spirit, unless we live to repent of our sins and to forgive others who violated us one way or the other. I pray this small book, help you change the way react to the slightest provocation, threat or violation against your life.

# CHAPTER 4
# ABOUT THE AUTHOR

Rev Franklin N Abazie is the founding and Presiding Pastor of Miracle of God Ministries with headquarters in Newark, New Jersey USA and a branch church in Owerri- Imo State Nigeria. He is following the footsteps of one of his mentors, Oral Roberts (Healing Evangelist) of the blessed memory.

The Lord passed Oral Roberts healing mantle two days before he went to be with the Lord at age 91 into the hand of healing evangelist-Rev Franklin N Abazie in a vision.

In all his services the Power and Presence of God is present to heal all in his audience. He is an ordained man of God with a Healing Ministry reviving the healing and miracle ministry of Jesus Christ of Nazareth.

Pastor Franklin N Abazie, is called by God with a unique mandate:

*"THE MOMENT IS DUE TO IMPACT YOUR WORLD THROUGH THE REVIVAL OF THE HEALING & MIRACLE MINISTRY OF JESUS CHRIST OF NAZARETH.*
*I AM SENDING YOU TO RESTORE HEALTH UNTO THEE AND I WILL HEAL THEE OF THY WOUNDS. SAID THE LORD OF HOST"*

He is a gifted ardent Teacher of the word of God who operates also in the office of a Prophet, generating and attracting undeniable signs & wonders, special miracles and healings, with apostolic fireworks of the Holy Ghost.

He is the founding and presiding senior Pastor of this fast growing Healing ministry.

## Chapter 4 - About the Author

He has written over 86 inspirational, healing and transforming books covering almost all aspect of divine healing and life. He is happily married and blessed with children.

# BOOKS BY REV FRANKLIN N ABAZIE

1) Commanding Abundance
2) The outcome of faith
3) Understanding the secret of prevailing prayers
4) Understanding the secret of the man God uses
5) Activating my due Season
6) Overcoming Divine Verdicts
7) The Outcome of Divine Wisdom
8) Understanding God's Restoration Mandate
9) Walking in the Victory and Authority of the truth
10) Gods Covenant Exemption
11) Destiny Restoration Pillars
12) Provoking Acceptable Praise
13) Understanding Divine Judgment
14) Activating Angelic Re-enforcement
15) Provoking Un-Merited Favor
16) The Benefits of the Speaking faith
17) Understanding Divine Arrangement

18) Understanding Divine Healing
19) The Mystery of Endurance
20) Obeying Divine Instructions
21) Understanding the Voice of God
22) Never give up on Hope
23) The prevailing Power of faith
24) Understanding Divine Prosperity
25) The Reward of Prayer
26) Covenant Keys to Answered Prayers
27) Activating the Forces of Vengeance
28) Put your faith to work
29) Where is your trust?
30) The Audacity of the Blood of Jesus
31) Redeeming Your Days
32) The force of Vision
33) Breaking the shackles of Family Curses
34) Wisdom for Marriage Stability
35) The winners Faith
36) The Prayer solution
37) The power of Prayer
38) Prayer strategy
39) The prayer that works
40) Walking in Forgiveness
41) The power of the grace of God

42) The power of Persistence
43) Overcoming Divine verdicts
44) The audacity of the blood of Jesus.
45) The prevailing power of the blood of Jesus
46) The benefit of the speaking faith.
47) Fearless faith
48) Redeeming Your Days.
49) The Supernatural Power of Prophecy
50) The companionship of the Holy Spirit
51) Understanding Divine Judgement
52) Understanding Divine Prosperity
53) Dominating Controlling Forces
54) The winners Faith
55) Destiny Restoration Pillars
56) Developing Spiritual Muscles
57) Inexplicable faith
58) The lifestyle of Prayer
59) Developing a positive attitude in life.
60) The mystery of Divine supply
61) Encounter with God's Power
62) Walking in love
63) Praying in the Spirit
64) How to provoke your testimony

65) Walking in the reality of the Anointing
66) The reality of new birth
67) The price of freedom
68) The Supernatural power of faith
69) The Power of Persistence
70) The intellectual components of Redemption
71) Overcoming Fear
72) The Force of Vision
73) Overcoming Prevailing Challenges
74) The Power of the Grace of God
75) My life & Ministry
76) The Mystery of Praise

**MIRACLE OF GOD MINISTRIES**

NIGERIA CRUSADE 2012

**MIRACLE OF GOD MINISTRIES**
NIGERIA CRUSADE 2012

**MIRACLE OF GOD MINISTRIES**

NIGERIA CRUSADE

2012

# MIRACLE OF GOD MINISTRIES

NIGERIA CRUSADE

2012

www.ingramcontent.com/pod-product-compliance
Lightning Source LLC
Chambersburg PA
CBHW021448080526
44588CB00009B/742